LUCAN
DE BELLO CIVILI VII

Revised from the edition of J. P. Postgate
by

O. A. W. Dilke
(Professor of Latin, University of Leeds)

Published by Bristol Classical Press
General Editor: John H. Betts

(by arrangement with Cambridge University Press)

First published by Cambridge University Press 1960

Reprinted with revised preface 1978, 1990, 2001 by
Bristol Classical Press
an imprint of
Gerald Duckworth & Co. Ltd
61 Frith Street
London W1D 3JL
E-mail: inquiries@duckworth-publishers.co.uk
Website: www.ducknet.co.uk

A catalogue record for this book is available
from the British Library

ISBN 0-906515-04-1

CONTENTS

PREFACE TO FIRST EDITION

Book VII of Lucan's historical epic on the civil
war covers the famous battle of Pharsalia, in which
Pompey was decisively defeated by Julius Caesar. This
edition of Book VII has been revised from that of the
late J. P. Postgate, Fellow of Trinity College, Cam-
bridge, Professor of Comparative Philology at Univer-
sity College, London, from 1880 to 1910, and Professor
of Latin at the University of Liverpool from 1909 to
1920. The revision has been made by kind permission
of his son Raymond Postgate and of the Cambridge Uni-
versity Press.

Both the introduction and the notes have been
considerably enlarged. A life of Lucan and other sec-
tions have been added to the introduction. Account
has been taken of some published criticisms of Post-
gate's edition by Professor W. B. Anderson. Some of
what Postgate wrote has been changed, comparatively
little omitted. His edition of 1896 underwent only
a slight revision in 1913, and the present revision
aims at making available to university students and
sixth-form pupils much of the scholarship of the last
sixty years. A. E. Housman's edition, which first
appeared in 1926, made an invaluable contribution to
the reading, punctuation and interpretation of the
text; it is only a pity that he did not study the
manuscripts in more detail. In 1928 a translation
by J. D. Duff, based very closely on Housman's text
and notes, was published in the Loeb series. The
Budé edition with French translation by A. Bourgery

v

and M. Ponchont (1926 and 1948), helpful in places
contains some curious errors. Recently Robert Graves's
translation has introduced Lucan to a wider circle;
but his English is too far from the Latin to help the
classical scholar and too often robs Lucan of his
rhetoric. For manuscript readings the third Teubner
edition (1913) of C. Hosius gives most help. C. E.
Haskins's annotated edition of 1887 is based on an
obsolete text; the best part of the book is the long
introduction by W. E. Heitland. Other editions of
Lucan which have appeared in the Pitt Press series
are those of Book I by R. J. Getty and of Book VIII
by J. P. Postgate.

I am indebted to C. J. Fordyce, Professor of
Humanity in the University of Glasgow, and H. H. Hux-
ley, Senior Lecturer in Latin in the University of
Manchester, for reading through my typescript and for
their helpful criticism, and to the latter for kindly
reading through the proofs. I am also indebted to
Professor G. B. A. Fletcher for a useful list of par-
allels, to Professor W. H. Semple for the purport of
the long note on *aethera contra* (line 2), and to Pro-
fessor E. C. Woodcock for a suggestion on lines 676 -
677. The librarians of the Bibliothèque Nationale,
Paris, and of the Bibliothèque Royale, Brussels, gave
me access to manuscripts of Lucan, and some of the
readings obtained from these have been incorporated
into the critical appendix. The two maps were kindly
drawn by my wife; in the second the numbering of battle-
lines is taken from F. L. Lucas's map.

The last section of the introduction deals with

vi

a controversial problem, the site of the battle of Pharsalia. Professor W. L. Gwatkin of the University of Missouri, with whom the Director of the British School at Athens put me in touch, kindly sent me, together with an offprint of his article, some helpful remarks and queries on this subject.

The consonantal *u* has not, as in most recent editions, been rendered as *v*. The retention of *u* is in accordance with Postgate's wishes, and it will be seen from the critical appendix on 658 that it illustrates a point of ambiguity.

GLASGOW   O.A.W.D.
May 1958

PREFACE TO BRISTOL CLASSICAL PRESS EDITION

There have, since the preface to the first edition, been two books in English on aspects of Lucan's poetry. M. P. O. Morford, *The Poet Lucan* (Oxford, 1967), gives a thorough analysis of his rhetorical technique, including sections on Alexander the Great, storms, divination and magic, and - of interest to readers of Book VII - dreams. Frederick M. Ahl, *Lucan: an Introduction* (Ithaca, New York, and London, 1976), gives comprehensive and often penetrating literary criticism; his latinity is sometimes suspect: indeed R. Mayer is only slightly exaggerating when he writes 'on page after page (Ahl) has failed to understand the text'.

vii

In French there is J. Brisset, *Les idées politiques de Lucain* (Paris, 1964). Fondation Hardt, *Entretiens sur l'antiquité classique* XV, ed. M. Durry (Vandoeuvres - Genève, 1970), has five contributions in French and two in German. Books in German are H. P. Syndikus, *Lucans Gedicht vom Bürgerkrieg: Untersuchungen zur epischen Technik und zu den Grundlagen des Werkes* (diss.: München, 1958); and more recently W. D. Lebek, *Lucans Pharsalia: Dichtungsstruktur und Zeitbezug* (Hypomnemata 44: Göttingen, 1976). A collection of essays in German (some in translation) is *Lucan*, ed. W. Rutz (Wege der Forschung 235: Darmstadt, 1970). In Italian there are two works by P. Tremoli: *M. Anneo Lucano, I: L'ambiente familiare e letterario* (Trieste, 1961) and *Religiosità e irreligiosità nel Bellum Civile di Lucano* (Trieste, 1968); also D. Gagliardi, *Lucano, poeta della libertà* (Napoli, 1958 and 2nd ed. 1970), and U. Piacentini, *Osservazioni sulla tecnica epica di Lucano* (Berlin, 1963).

Neronians and Flavians: Silver Latin I, ed. D. R. Dudley (London and Boston, 1972), contains two chapters by the present editor, 'Lucan's Political Views and the Caesars' and 'Lucan and English literature'. The poet's legacy is also covered by H.-D. Leidig, *Das Historiengedicht in der englischen Literaturtheorie: Die Rezeption von Lucans Pharsalia von der Renaissance bis zum Ausgang des achtzehnten Jahrhunderts* (Bern and Frankfurt/M, 1975), and by E. Paratore, *Dante e Lucano* (Torino, 1962).

More detailed studies are O. Schönberger, *Untersuchungen zur Wiederholungstechnik Lucans* (2nd ed.:

viii

München, 1968); A. Ollfors, *Studien zum Aufbau des Hexameters Lucans* and *Textkritische und interpretatorische Beiträge zu Lucan* (Göteborg, 1967); H. C. Gotoff, *The Transmission of the Text of Lucan in the Ninth Century* and Vivian Holliday, *Pompey in Cicero's Correspondence and Lucan's* Civil War (The Hague and Paris, 1969).

Book VII has been edited with Italian notes by D. Gagliardi (Firenze, 1975). The mediaeval commentator Arnulf has been edited by Berthe M. Marti (Papers and Monographs of the American Academy at Rome, No. 18: Rome, 1958) - but the edition is wordy and shows much ignorance. A German prose translation, with appendix, has been published by W. Ehlers (München, 1973). The present author has translated Book VII into English verse: *The Battle of Pharsalia* (Leeds Philosophical and Literary Society: Leeds, 1971).

Some points of textual criticism are commented on by D. R. Bradley in *Latomus* 28 (1969) 175 - 185; R. Braun in *Annales de la Faculté des Lettres et Sciences humaines de Nice* 11 (1970) 121 - 130; M. Erren in *Hermes* 91 (1963) 74 - 103; K. von Fritz in *Hermes* 103 (1975) 251 - 252; A. Hudson-Williams in *Boll. Stud. Lat.* 2 (1972) 49; D. A. Kidd in *Mnemosyne* 19 (1966) 42 - 45; L. Koenen in *Rhein. Mus.* 107 (1964) 190 - 192; Carolyne J. Matzke in *Mnemosyne* 22 (1969) 181 - 5; G. Perrotta in *Studi Urbinati* 39, 1 (1965) 7 - 17; R. Verdière in *Latomus* 30 (1971) 723 - 726; and M. Zicàri in *Bull. Assoc. G. Budé* (1959) 516. Most of the many articles on the literary criticism of Lucan's poem will be found in Ahl's or Gagliardi's bibliography.

LEEDS
August 1978

O.A.W.D.

ADDENDA AND CORRIGENDA

Page 74, in line 659: for "'*parcite iam, superi,*"read
"'*parcite*', *ait, 'superi.*"

Page 87, note on 28: for "possessor" read "person in-
terested".

Page 125, note on 395, line 4: for "moveable" read
"movable".

Page 126, note on 406: for "*tanto in tempore*" and
what follows read "*tanto in corpore* - Rome's in-
creased population".

Page 167, note on 21 - 26, line 3: for "Artemidorous"
read "Artemidorus".

Page 176, under Cato Uticensis: add 40 n. 2.